Frugal Living

Make Your Money Go Further

Introduction

Welcome to "Frugal Living- Make your Money Go Further"

After working in the finance sector for many years and realizing that in general, we as a population waste far more than we need to, I started to think about how I could get this message out there.

I have worked with so many people and families that had got themselves into financial difficulties, going into debt and such when it could have been avoided.

In this book I discuss some of the many strategies you can use to not only increase your income but to dramatically decrease your outgoings.

Learn how to cut your shopping bill in half, save like a pro and increase your income with a freelance, home based job as well as many other useful topics such as where to find the best deals and coupon codes.

I hope that this book makes a positive difference to your life so that you can start using some of your spare funds on important things like spending quality time out with family.

Table of Contents

Chapter 1

Increase Your Income

We all need a little extra money every now and then. Between emergencies and the always imminent gift-giving season, there is always a reason to need a little extra cash.

Luckily, The rise of online freelancer markets such as Upwork, Uber, and Fiverr have made it even easier for people to do some extra jobs on the side. These sites allow you to offer your skills such as writing, proofreading, voice over work, researching, data entry or many other things from the comfort of your own home and get paid for it!

Last year, a survey done by the Freelancers Union concluded that over 53 million Americans qualify and work as freelancers by doing online freelancing work as part time or even full time jobs. 14.3 million people consider themselves to be "moonlighters", meaning that they have a day job that pays benefits while they work with consulting or freelancing on the side to increase their earnings each month.

It's an easy and fantastic way to bring in a few extra pennies.

How to Get a Freelance Job
Getting a freelance job isn't as hard as it may seem. However, if you want to find a job that best suits your lifestyle and your passions, you have to take some precautions.

1) Have the right frame of mind.
You don't have to have a degree in different fields to be able to work in freelance. That being said, just because you don't have a degree, doesn't mean that you can't follow your passion. For example, let's take freelance writing, which is a big and growing field. When I think of writing, a lot of different jobs come to mind:

- Blogging
- Writing web content
- Writing non-fiction ebooks
- Writing short stories or novellas
- Ghostwriting
- Scriptwriting
- Songwriting
- Writing slogans
- Writing greeting card sentiments

- Editing
- Researching term papers
- Writing correspondence

And that's just the tip of the iceberg. Not only do the projects vary in type, they also vary in topic. Do you bake for a living? You can write about baking. Are you an accountant? You could be a tutor, a consultant, write eBooks about finance, etc. The only limit to your projects is your imagination and your expertise.

One thing that you do need to remember is that this side project – your part time job – is something that you need to love. You work a day job because it pays the bills, has benefits, and (if you're lucky) you're fond of. This side job will provide extra income but it should also provide you with happiness. You are giving up some of your free time to work so you should be happy while you do that work.

2) find out what you want to do and what your passion is.

The next step is to go out and find out what your passion is. Everyone has a passion in their lives. Some of us just haven't found out what that is just yet. If you're one of those people who haven't found that passion yet, don't fret. In fact, you're in a fantastic spot. Think of it as a clean slate.

Take a weekend to yourself, if you are able. If you can't, spend a Sunday afternoon by yourself to gather your thoughts and reflect on some important details.

The first thing that you need to do is to find where your values lie. When you do this, you'll be able to get to the root of what drives you. Make a list of values that you find essential to living the life that you want. Don't worry about how long the list is. Do you find intellect to be important? What about creativity? Or do you enjoy helping people?

Although this may seem like an odd task at this stage, it will enable you to reach out to the right people when looking for freelance work.

3) Check out the latest resources.

There are many different sites that you can go to in order to find that side job. Even before you do your own personal, internal research, go ahead and check out some of these sites to see what is out there. My two big suggestions are:

- Upwork (formerly known as oDesk)
- Craigslist

Beyond that, check out some of these other sites:

- Freelancer
- Fiverr
- Gigblasters
- Guru
- RapidWorkers
- People Per Hour
- Smashing Jobs
- Taskr
- Just Answer
- Job Boy
- Short Task
- TenBux
- Tutor
- Workhoppers
- YunoJuno
- Zeerk

4) Be patient and be organized.

It's not going to happen overnight. You're going to have to be patient when it comes to getting new gigs and clients, especially if you haven't gotten your foot in the door yet. It always takes a while to get momentum when you're starting from scratch.

Keeping organized is a great suggestion but there are so many different ways to stay organized, it almost feels as helpful as saying "Just do it." Just do what? So to be more helpful, I want to give you a couple of different options. I stay organized by using a combination of a digital calendar that syncs with my phone and a hardcopy daily planner that sits on my desk.

I use my daily planner for tasks and reminders of events. If I have an upcoming deadline or a string of small tasks that need to be completed, I write them down in there so that I don't forget the small things (and the big looming things in the future). I use my digital calendar for items that involve others. If I have an event that I have invited others to, I use a community Google calendar (which I've shared with them). I also add yearly reminders like birthdays, tax dates, anniversaries, holidays, and quarterly evaluations in that calendar. My phone is synced to it so I get reminders a week in advance.

This system works for me. If you think it might work for you, try it out.

5) Network and keep up with contacts.

Networking is like marketing. You need to keep up with it if you want it to help you with your side business. When you're starting from scratch and you're trying to gain momentum, your biggest tool will be "word of mouth". Do you want to knit baby blankets as your side job? That's great! You should find some conventions, workshops, or meetups. Find a knitting group. There, you can learn more about your craft and you can make contacts if you need to look for clientele or advice on how to move forward with your specific craft.

That being said, not everyone likes to network. Not only that, for those who haven't needed to network in the past, it might seem like an ominous task to start on. If this sounds like you, check out some of these helpful tips to get you started:

- **Ask the right questions.** When you are networking, you may be afraid of not knowing what to say. That's pretty normal.

If you're not used to promoting yourself, you might be at a loss as to where to start. There are three questions that you should really focus on when you are in a networking situation:

- o What ideas can you get from others?
- o How can you help other people?
- o Who else can you talk to? Or who else can help you develop your business?

- **Reconnect with some friends and family members.** You already have a fan base out of your past and current relationships.

- **Try to rearrange your furniture.** I'm serious, it works! Sometimes, how your office (or where you will be setting up shop) is set up, you unintentionally hole yourself up in a small corner. Instead, try reaching out by moving your furniture so that you'll be interacting with more people. Will you be setting up shop at home? Why not try working somewhere else sometimes? If you're a knitter, writer, or artist, try going to a café to work at least once a week. If it is sunny, go out to a park and work at one of those benches or picnic tables. Get yourself out there!

- **Set up a "Meeting New People" fund.** We don't all have the extra money to go to conferences or conventions. If you write on the side, those writing conventions can cost a fortune! So, why not keep a jar in your kitchen where you can drop your lose change. Even if you don't want to spend the money to go to a conference, you can use this money to take a class in your new field or buy dinner at a meetup group.

Chapter 2

Couponing 101

The term "couponing" has changed throughout the years. As things have gotten more expensive and as we've begun to acquire more things, the need for using coupons has been more and more of a trend. In fact, there are now, four levels of couponing from someone who occasionally clips coupons to someone who can be considered an "Extreme Couponer". Have you seen the TV shows? Yes, this is real. Yes, you can do that too, if you have the time and desire.

Each level of couponing has different tendencies and practices in order for that level of a couponer to be successful.

Casual Clipper

Most people would be considered a casual clipper. This means that you clip coupons when you see one that interests you in the newspaper. To be considered in this category, you probably clip less than 10 coupons for a trip to the groceries. You'll save a few bucks in the process. The savings in this category is pretty minimal but pennies soon grow into pounds!

Generic Shopper

For this category (level II), you would need to shop and buy a generic brand when faced with the name brand because of the price comparison. If you only buy generic brands, you can actually save a large chunk of change. I'm talking hundreds of dollars a month for a family of four.

The only problem with this that sometimes the name brand performs better than generic brands. During times like these, you don't end up saving the money, especially if you need to buy more of the generic product to equal the quality level of the name brand stuff.

Deal Shopper

I am seeing more and more people fall under this category. If you want to be a deal shopper, who things come into play:

1. You only shop and buy things that are on sale.

2. You use a coupon on these items as well.

This will double your savings (or more) and there are plenty of other types of savings with this technique as well. I have seen many couponers who have quickly risen to this level or rank of shopper and it has saved them tons of money. The only problem is that sometimes:

- The best deal comes with having to buy in bulk, which won't cost more but will be troublesome to store

- You have to travel to various stores in order to get the best deal.

- You may need something specific that is not on sale. Once you get used to sale prices, it feels horrible having to buy something at full price.

This technique is simple but it does take some getting used to. For example, let's say that you see a specific name brand body wash on sale for $0.99

about once a month or so for about a week. Once you see that pattern, you can start looking for coupons for that brand. If you have a $0.50 cents off coupon for that product, you can buy it for $0.49 cents! That's a much better deal than buying the generic brand!

Of course, this only really works if you have the time and patience that it takes to look for the deals and look for the coupons.

Extreme Couponer

These people know that you can use both an in-store coupon and a manufacturer's coupon at the same time. Did you know that you could do that? Well, now you do. Being able to use both of these coupons on an item that is already at a deal (let's say a BOGO – buy one, get one sale) is great, especially if you have two sets of coupons for each item.

Believe it or not, some of these extreme couponers even leave the store with extra money in their pockets. Yes, that is extreme! Sometimes, the big problem with extreme couponing is that people who do this let it take over their lives. You don't have to let it take over your life. Just stay vigilante for sales and spend one afternoon clipping coupons.

All right, now let's talk about some specific examples, shall we?

Gather Your Supplies.

There are some great coupon inserts that come in the paper. The most common ones are "Red Plum" and "Smart Source". If you don't get these in the paper (or if you don't get the paper), you can go online and print directly from their website. I also suggest checking out coupons.com. If you want to look for even more coupons check out some of these ideas:

- Get them directly from the various manufacturers that you frequent. You can either go on their website or contact them to request some coupons.

- You can find some coupons on the packaging. Don't forget to take a second look at the label to see if there are some coupons on the reverse side of the label.

- In your junk mail. Some high-value manufacturers have started to send their coupons through the mail so check out your junk mail before you get rid of them.

Keep Your Supplies Organized

Some big time couponers suggest keeping a binder with baseball card sleeves and divider tabs. That would be one of the most organized ways to keep your coupons in order. You can either tab them by expiration date or by product type.

The key to keeping them organized is to find the approach you will get the most out of. You can either clip all of the coupons that you get, and organize all of them – just in case you need one. You can cut out the coupons that you only intend to use. The last option is to keep all of the coupons intact on the page and file them away, cutting them out as you run across those products.

I have two ways of organizing my coupons. I keep all of the coupons that I run across and go through them each Sunday with the local store ads. I match up sale items with coupons for those products, cut them out, and file them in my binder. When I go grocery shopping, I take out the ones that I intend to use and put them in a small accordion container (made for coupons). I divide them up by store instead of by product type and then go to each store and buy the products that are on sale (and that I have a coupon for) all in one day.

Learn about Your Favorite Store's Coupon Policy

Not every store has the same type of coupon policy. Some coupons will let you use manufacturer coupons in addition to store coupons. Some will only let you use coupons on items that are not on sale. Here is a convenient list of links to common stores and their coupon policies: http://frugalliving.about.com/od/coupons andrebates/qt/Store-Coupon-Policies.htm

Once You Know the Rules, Get Creative

You have to make sure not to abuse those rules because if you annoy the cashiers and managers, they won't be so kind to you when you walk through that door. Here are some clever ways to get more coupons and get the most out of them:

- If you're traveling on a Sunday, check out the newspaper inserts from different regions. They will (most likely) be different and you will also find different ads for different stores.

- If you find a specific set of coupons that you really like, buy multiple papers so that you can get more of that coupon. An extra paper may cost you another couple of dollars but if those two coupons could save you more than ten dollars or so, I would say that the extra cost is worth it.

- Did you know that you can combine a buy- one- get- one- free sale with buy- one- get- one- free coupons too! Just make sure that your specific store doesn't frown upon that. If you find a store that will let you do that, you've just hit the jackpot!

- A lot of stores will accept their competitor's coupons. Just ask the cashier as they ring you up.

Keep track of which stores tell you that you that their policy is to accept any coupons.

- Coupons still work on clearance items. Score!

- Many grocery cards will let you add coupons to them. This is a great way to save money without having to carry a ton of coupons around with you. Just make sure that you keep track of the manufacturer's coupons that you put on your card so you don't accidentally use the same print coupon during checkout. That can get confusing.
That being said, electronic coupons are pretty awesome. You can get them onto your grocery loyalty card. You can even get them onto your cell phones. Some stores have apps that let you download coupons.

- One of my pet peeves is that most of the coupons that you run into when you are searching for a good deal, are for processed foods. You don't see a lot of coupons for healthy and organic foods. However, there are a few printable coupon sites that specialize in foods that are healthy for you – not just prepackaged foods. Check out mambosprouts.com and betterforyou.com/active-offers for some coupons on items that help you get and stay healthy.

- Check out some mommy blogs and deal/frugal blogs and subscribe to them. If you find one that you like (bonus points if they live a lifestyle that mimics yours), they'll probably let you know of some great deals in real time. Check out organicdeals.com or coupondivas.com as a couple of examples to get you started.

Chapter 3

Creative Savings

I know saving money may seem difficult but in reality, it's all about perspective and determination. Remember that even the little things count. If you're looking for some money saving tips that you can slowly incorporate into your life, you're going to find them in this chapter.

These tips are great for saving a little money here and there and chances are, you won't even see that much of a change in your lifestyle. As important as it is to save this money, it is equally as important to know where to put it. Where will you put all of the money that you save? A savings account? A jar for money towards a vacation or holiday presents? Do you have a different bank account for different things? A joint account with your spouse to pay bills?

Having a goal (whether it's to save your loose change all year long and spend that money on Christmas presents or if you want to put $100 more dollars into your savings account each month) is important. Not only is it one of the only ways to track your progress, it is also a way to track your habits. Generally speaking, when you start saving money, you start making healthier decisions.

1. Let Go of Cable.

One of the best ways to save money is to cut back on your bills by either eliminating you cable bill all together or switch to a cheaper plan. This will also help you save on your electric bill and your phone rental. You can use this extra money to cover some other expenses or put the money that you save into your savings.

2. Sell What You're Not Using

Garage sales may seem like a silly summer project but you can make a few dollars by selling your unwanted things in garage sales, to secondhand stores, on Craigslist, eBay, or refurbishing them to look new or repurposed and selling them on Etsy. You can even turn this into a second income if you know what you're doing. If you don't want to spend all of your spare time on this, consider having this be a family project just before a vacation or in preparation for the upcoming holiday season.

3. Save Money By Utilizing the 30-Day Rule

Instant gratification is one of the main reasons why people run into money problems. The 30-Day Rule can help you with this. The rule is simple; when you find something that you can't live without, wait 30 days to decide whether or not this purchase is that important. Of course, this doesn't apply to things like groceries but it does apply to less important things like that purse that you've been eyeing, the watch that you "need", at sale item on Amazon, etc. Most of the time, after you've waited for a month, you'll find that you don't have that urge to buy it any longer. Meaning that you've just saved yourself some money by waiting. It really makes you think about what is important and what's worth your hard earned money.

4. Don't Go Shopping Without a List

Of course, the key to this is to actually stick to the list and not veering away from it. When you're at home, you know what you need but when you get to the store, you're tempted by so many different things – even grocery shopping. No those Oreos aren't necessary for you or your diet and neither is that 50 gallon drum of cheesy poofs.

5. A Different Way to Be Social

One of the things that people think about when they hear the words "save money" or "on a budget" is the fact that they won't be able to have fun anymore. That's utter baloney. You just have to find different ways to be social. Instead of going out to the bar, invite some of your friends over for a movie. You can also host a dinner where everyone can pitch-in for ingredients or dishes. You can have poker night with your friends. All of this is much cheaper than going out to eat or going clubbing.

6. Entertaining Your Kids

Unlike what they may try to tell you, they don't need the latest toys to be happy and entertained. Sure, some things can really help them grow intellectually, but you can do that while you are on a budget as well.

Instead of buying them new books, take them to the library once a week. The library has movies as well. You can buy second hand toys instead of brand new ones. You can also save money by having them make their own toys. Kids are resourceful and smart. Their imaginations are amazing and they thrive if you will let them. Have a recycle bin of safe items that they can repurpose by using some craft supplies and their imaginations.

7. Stay Properly Hydrated

Drinking water will save you money and add years to your life. If you drink a big glass of water before you eat a meal, you'll be more likely to eat less and stay full longer. You will also save money on soda and other types of drinks if you drink more water. Use a reusable water bottle instead of bottled water. You will also save on medical bills in the future if you are properly hydrated. And remember, tap water is clean and "free".

8. for Goodness Sakes, Read More

Not only will your kids benefit from a library card, you will as well. I won't go into the hundreds of ways that reading can benefit your physical and mental health. I'll just go into the financial benefits. Libraries make entertainment virtually free. You have an unlimited amount of books at your disposal and the only money that you have to spend is for the gas to get there and back (and maybe an occasional late fee).

If you have an ereader, you can use a program like Overdrive to rent and borrow ebooks and audiobooks from the library. You don't even have to pay for the gas to get you to the library! Sure the newest books might not be available as quickly but there are thousands of books that you haven't read yet, which are just as entertaining.

9. Every Little Bit

Putting away fifty cents a day doesn't seem like much but if you do, that's nearly $250 a year. Even the tiniest savings can add up. Just imagine what you can do if you put a dollar in a jar.

10. Health Bills

Taking good care of yourself doesn't sound like a good way to save money. Sure, it's good for you but how can it be good for your finances? Health bills are the most expensive and can be the most earth shattering expenses that you will run across – especially if you don't have an emergency fund set up. Practice good preventative care. Stop smoking. Take good care of your teeth. Drink plenty of water. Go to your yearly checkups and follow the advice of your doctor. It pays to practice good preventative care.

Exercise more. Yes, it's something that most people don't want to do but it will save you money on your health related bills. You don't have to spend money at the gym either. Practice stretching and yoga at home. Take a walk or a jog every day. Double up on this time by taking care of yourself and spending time with your family. When you walk your dog, go out with your kids as well. Go for a walk around the block and spend some quality time together. Play games at the park. Organize it into an inexpensive social event: a game of flag football, capture the flag, or dodgeball. It is a fun way to stay in shape and hang out with the people that you care about.

11. Assess Your Clothing Purchases

You might think that buying an inexpensive shirt will save you money if you're forgoing a more expensive shirt.

The reasoning seems right but you have to make sure to look at the quality as well. Two inexpensive shirts won't last you as long as a more expensive one if you have to keep buying the same item over and over again, especially for work. Look at the fabric, the washability, the stitching, and other quality factors when you pick up clothes.

Also look at how you have to take care of your clothing. Dry cleaning bills add up fairly quickly. If you can clean your quality clothes inexpensively, they're the better option. Washing and ironing your clothes yourself can save you hundreds of dollars a year.

Chapter 4

Repurposing and Upcycling

Repaint It!

It is amazing what a new coat of paint will do for your furniture and even for your walls. Whenever I want a big change in my home (I used to be a nomad so − for me - staying in one place can see like a drag after a while) I repaint the walls and rearrange my furniture. It is great because it makes the whole place feel like it's brand new and the only thing that you have to buy is the paint!

Reupholster

Want some new furniture? After a while your comfortable but tired couch may look like it wants to be put out of its misery. A couple of YouTube videos and supplies is all it may take to bring some new life into it. Hobby shops like Joann Fabrics and local shops always send coupons in the mail if you sign up for their mailing program. No cost to you − just a couple of extra pieces of mail every month. Joann also sends out coupons via text message. A "60% off a regularly priced item" coupon gets sent out every couple of months. Those come in handy if you go into the store and find that the perfect fabric isn't on sale.

Repurpose

If you're looking for new furniture, take a good look at the furniture that you're not currently using. Have you been wanting to get rid of something for a while?

- Maybe an old bookshelf can be turned into an adult bar.
- Turn an old picture frame into a serving tray for your spouse or for guests.
- Old suitcases can be turned into interesting dog beds or even a medicine cabinet.
- Old doors can be turned into tabletops.
- Bulletin boards can be made into a jewelry organizer.
- Books can be mounted with brackets to make interesting shelves.
- Blank CD storage cases can be turned into other types of storage, like organizing cables in the garage.

- Old shower hooks (the S ring kind) can be used in your closet to hang bags scarves, or ties.
- Hanging shoe racks can be used to organize your pantry, cleaning supplies, or toys for your kids' rooms.

All you need is a little ingenuity and creativity to turn your old items into a unique conversation starter with multiple purposes.

Chapter 5

Make don't Buy

There are a number of things that you can make at home instead of buying at the store. Often, people will pay for convenience. Instead of having to make a cleanser, they will pay for a bottle of scented cleanser. The product works great but at around eight dollars a bottle, you can make something from home for cheaper. For example, since we were talking about scented cleansers, let's use that recipe.

Using an eighth of a cup of your favorite fabric softener, a couple tablespoons of baking soda, an empty spray bottle, and some hot tap water, you can make a product that is comparable to the name brand product! Let's check out some other products shall we?

Carpet Refresher

You can use baking soda all around your house. It's not just for cooking. My favorite application is to use it to help refresh my carpets and rug. I sprinkle it around and leave it overnight. Then, I vacuum it up in the morning. I make sure that my pets are kept in another room so that they don't accidentally lap all of it up before I can get to it with the vacuum cleaner. It helps gets out stains and the smells that are associated with owning a pet and really living in a home.

I also use it to brighten up my stainless steel appliances in the kitchen and to help scrub my counters if I find a coffee or tea stain. Make a paste out of baking soda and warm water, then scrub the stain using the paste and a paper towel.

You can find large bags of baking soda in the cleaning department of most big box stores. The baking soda in these bags are cleaning grade, which means that the granular aren't made for cooking. You can use kitchen grade baking soda but it wouldn't be the best to cook with the bulk baking soda that you find in the cleaning department.

Dog Treats
It is much healthier and cost effective to make dog treats instead of buying them. Here are some great (and simple) recipes to try. Before you start to make treats for your little furry friends, make sure that you keep a close

eye on them and check their medical records for any known allergies.

One of my favorite recipes is the absolute easiest: **Natural Homemade Sweet Potato Chews**. Bigger dogs will make mincemeat out of these in about five minutes but it is still a healthy treat that will keep them occupied for a little bit of time. Smaller dogs will take more time. This is a great option in lieu of pig ear chews, which can be dangerous if they choke on a large chunk. While pig ears can run up to about $2 each, these sweet potato chews can be made for just pennies each!

Just take a sweet potato, wash it thoroughly, then slice them into pieces that are about a fourth to a third of an inch wide. Plop them onto a piece of parchment paper lined baking sheet and stick them in a 250 degree oven for about three hours. You're going to want to make sure that they are dry and chewy so flip them over at the halfway mark and inspect them. They may need to go in for a bit longer if needed.

Store them in the refrigerator or freezer. They will be good for about two weeks but I bet that your furry family members will go through them faster than that!

Dogs love peanut butter. Pumpkin is great for their digestive tracts. Why not combine them in this recipe for **Pumpkin and Peanut Butter Dog Biscuits**?

For this one you're going to need two and a half cups of flour (preferably whole wheat since it is better for your furry buddies), a couple of eggs, three fourths of a cup of pumpkin puree, and three tablespoons of natural peanut butter. Preheat your oven for 350 degrees and mix all of the ingredients together until it forms a big ball. On a floured surface, roll it out until it is about a fourth of an inch thick.

Using your favorite cookie cutter, cut out the biscuits and place them onto a cookie sheet that is coated with cooking spray. I have a silicone mat, that I absolutely love, which eliminates the need for the cooking spray. If you have parchment paper, you won't need the cooking spray either. Bake for about a half an hour. Watch your first batch to make sure that you don't burn them (since every oven is different).

One of my go-to favorites is for **Two Ingredient Doggie Biscuits**. All you have to do is take a small container of baby food (make sure that it doesn't have ingredients that will make your poor pup sick, like any kind of onions for example), and a cup of whole wheat flour. My dog likes the chicken and sweet potato baby food biscuits especially.

The dough is always really sticky so you'll need to flour your surfaces and the rolling pin. And your hands. And the cookie cutter... However, the ingredients are cheap and it is fairly easy. Just bake them in a 350 degree oven (sprayed pan, on a silicone mat, or on parchment paper) for about 20 to 25 minutes.

You can keep them in a cookie canister if you want to keep them a little on the chewy or softer side. If you like hard biscuits, keep them in a paper bag. They keep for about two weeks but make sure to watch for mold after about a week.

As far as dog food goes, it is also cheaper and healthier for your dog since you will be feeding him less preservatives but it does take more time to make dog food fresh every couple days. I say "every couple days" because fresh food doesn't last as long as dry kibble or canned food. However, if you want to try it out, I suggest keeping these things in mind:

1. Make sure that you grind up the vegetables in the food really well.
2. Make sure that you vary the type of foods that they get in their food while maintaining a healthy ratio.
3. Consider mixing in a nutritional supplement like fish oil to help make sure that they're getting everything that they need out of their food.
4. Double and triple check the ingredients to make sure that you don't give your dog a food that will make him sick. Onions, grapes, raisins, avocado, alcohol, caffeine, garlic (I've heard that it is both good and bad for your dog but I would suggest consulting your vet first), candy, gum, chocolate, fat trimmings, etc. Check with your vet for a full list.
5. Keep in mind that brown rice is much healthier than white rice
6. Broccoli and cauliflower isn't bad in moderation but watch out for

gastric discomfort and upset tummies.

Presents and Gifts

Buying present and gifts (especially around the holidays) can add up to a lot of money. There are many things that you can make for someone as a gift. The first thing that you have to keep in mind when it comes to homemade gifts is to **make it personalized**. The great thing about homemade gifts is that since you spend time making each one, you can personalize each with your own specific flair.

While it is cheaper to make something in bulk (baking cookies for everyone, crafting candles for everyone, or bottling hand or body scrubs, for example), some people just don't want something like that. While I know that I can make sugar scrubs for my sister-in-law and her daughter, my brother wouldn't be so thrilled with that present. He would much prefer homemade cookies in the shape of footballs.

The second thing you have to remember is to **make a list**. Yes, like Santa Claus. Since you are personalizing some gifts, it is important to keep them all straight. For example, this year, I may decide to make sugar scrubs for a third of my loved ones, bake cookies for another third, and then sew crafts for the last third.

Another thing to remember is to **start as early as you can**. The earlier you start, the less stress you will be. In addition to that, you can also spend the time to wait for sales to happen. Let's say that you're a knitter. If you wait until November to start knitting mittens for all of your kids and grandkids, you may end up paying through the nose for just the right yarn unless you are lucky enough to find a sale. If you start in the summer, you have months to snag up just the right yarn at the right price.

Chapter 6

Cutting Your Grocery Bill In Half

One of the biggest reoccurring bills (other than your mortgage or loans) might end up being your grocery bill if you don't shop during sales or with coupons. I've come up with this list of tips to help you cut that grocery bill in half. Some of them might seem overtly easy but they are usually overlooked because of the effort involved. A little time and elbow grease can save you money. Don't underestimate that. Here are 30 tips to help you save money when you're out buying groceries.

1. Follow your list. You have to go into the store with a plan and you have to stick to that plan. Before you go, take a look at the grocery ads that you get in the mail. Check out the deals and price match to make sure that you are getting the best deal on items. If you can keep from impulse buying items, you can save a lot of cash. In fact, keeping a running list on your refrigerator door can help you keep track of what you really need.

2. Do you know what a rain check is? If a store advertises a product that is on sale but have run out of that item, you can go to the customer service counter and request a "rain check". When they restock that item, they'll let you buy the advertised item at that sale price, even if the sale is over.

3. What comes first? Buy the items that are on sale and then plan your meals around them. I like to create my shopping list based on the sale items, look online for recipes, and then plan my meals for the week. After that, I go to the store.

4. Never shop when you are hungry. You'll be more tempted to make impulse buys if that happens.

5. Check the unit price of the items. I leave this to my spouse when we shop together. A name brand item might be on sale, but sometimes, the generic brand may be cheaper in the long run. You can check this by looking at the unit price, which is the price for one unit of whatever it is you are looking to buy.

6. Pay attention to what you buy and what the "regular" price is for that item. Often, we'll be so impulsive when something says "SALE" that we won't realize that it is really a terrible deal!

7. Stocking up on items that you buy often, when they are on sale is really worth it. Even if an item is perishable, if you are able to preserve it when you get home, it can be worth it. For example, if you buy bread at a special price, you can freeze the extra loaves until you need it. The same goes with vegetables. Just make sure that you check the freezer before you go out and buy some more.

8. Grow your own vegetables, if you can. Herbs are a great way to start if you've never really grown any vegetables or plants before. Most herbs are hearty and will hold up to a little neglect or abuse. They also taste better than the dried and powdered versions.

9. Cook at home. Buying fast food or buying frozen items might save you some time and energy but

cooking your own meals will actually be healthier, taste better, and is cheaper in the long run.

10.   Make leftovers interesting. Having leftover chicken might sound boring or tedious but you can really spice it up by looking for leftover recipes online. For example, leftover meat at our house, usually ends up in a fried rice dish the next day. Leftover chicken tastes great in a rice, cheese, and broccoli casserole.

11. Need some specialty items? Believe it or not, shopping around online might be your best bet. Amazon has some great, unique bulk foods which are cheaper than at local specialty stores. One great example is with coconut oil and coconut flour.

12. Support your local farmers by checking out the farmer's market. The prices are better and you'll be helping out some great, hardworking people.

13. Drug stores are great places to find some deals. However, you have to make sure to check out

their weekly deals. Items that aren't on sale are usually overpriced.

14. Getting a membership at a grocery store is free and can be beneficial when their "specially priced" items go on sale. Even club membership stores that sell in bulk can come in handy if you have a big family. Items that are usually sold in bulk have cheaper per unit prices than their smaller counterparts.

15. Items which are not food (like toilet paper, shampoo, and soap) are often cheaper at big box stores.

16. Dollar Store items may seem cheap but their quality is often lacking. However, there are some items that you can buy there without having to look twice:

    a. Wax paper
    b. Cotton swabs
    c. Double sided tape (but try to stay away from the off-brands)
    d. Parchment paper

e. Holiday decorations
f. Mailing labels
g. Shaving cream
h. Sandwich and storage bags
i. Boxed candy (like movie theater candy)
j. Socks
k. Trays and plastic containers
l. Balloons
m. Bleach
n. Peroxide
o. Dental floss
p. Goo Gone
q. Stocking stuffers
r. Stemware, glasses and other tableware
s. Petroleum jelly
t. Dermasil body lotion

17. Go through your pantry once every couple weeks. We end up throwing away so many things that expire because we forget about them. Taking stock of what you have is important to do so that you don't waste your hard earned paychecks.

18. Only go to grocery shopping once a week – at the max. The less shopping you do, the more money you will save. It

will help you reduce the money that you spend on impulse buys.

19. Go through your last grocery receipt and find the five most expensive items. Now try to find cheaper substitutes for those items. You may be able to find generic brands or a different type of the same item. For example, ground turkey is often cheaper than ground beef.

20. Pick out ten items that you buy most often. Go to the big stores in your area and compare the regular price of those items. Making a spreadsheet will often help. The point is to find the store with the lowest overall price for your most common needs.

21. Download coupons. You don't have go get a subscription to a newspaper. Instead, download them from coupons.com, redplum.com, or smartsource.com. Before you use them, wait until those items are on sale so that you can double up on your savings.

22.   Think ahead when it comes to sales. Sales generally run on an eight to twelve week rotation, meaning that if you see something on sale now, you won't see it go on sale again for either to twelve weeks. So let's say that you see cereal on sale for a dollar a box. If you know that your kids go through a box of cereal a week, buy about ten weeks' worth while it is on sale.

23.   Know the layouts of the stores that you frequent. If you make a grocery list and you know where everything is, you won't have to walk up and down every aisle, which means that you'll be less exposed to things that you may buy on an impulse.

24.   If you can go shopping on your own, do so. You'll be less likely to make purchases that you don't need if you go by yourself.

25.   If you're only going to the store for a handful of products for the week, don't get a huge cart. Just get a small basket or one of those half- sized carts instead. The more space that you have,

the more tempted you will be to buy the things that you don't need. Don't give yourself the free space to fill your cart with impulse buy items.

26.   Let's say that something is not on sale but you need it: like a bottle of ketchup. Instead of looking straight ahead at the shelf that is in front of you, look above and below the shelf to see what those prices are. That's where you will normally find items that are on sale and less expensive brands.

27.   Go through the self-checkout. When you do, you won't be standing in line in front of those impulse buy candy and magazine racks. When you're busy checking yourself out, you'll be less likely to spend money on those last minute buys at the register: gum, candy, peperoni sticks, magazines, 20 ounce bottles of soda, chap stick, snack sized baggies of junk food, etc.

28.   Don't buy prepackaged food items. Buy things in bulk, and then divide them up at home. The

most common example is cheese. Instead of buying sliced cheddar, buy the block and then cut slices at home. This will save you money, even though it might take a bit of extra time when you get home.

29.   Buy the produce that's in season. You'll save around 50% on the price of produce if you buy the fruits and veggies that are in season. Besides, that will help you and your kids vary the types of vegetables that you eat each month.

30.   Buy meat in bigger packs. Did you know that if you buy meat in bulk (let's say 40 pounds), you can get it at a fraction of the cost? Often your local butcher will offer these kind of packages or if not there are many resources online. It's a great way to buy meat at an inexpensive cost. If you don't have an extra freezer to store the meat, split the cost with a friend or family member and then divide the meat up amongst yourselves.

31. Take lunch with you! One of the biggest spends I found when working in a 9-5 is lunch. Even pre packaged sandwiches can add up to a hefty some every day and don't get me started on meeting the girls for lunch at the local café!

I now take my own lunch, which allows me to control the calories as well as the cost, and on a fine day I will arrange to meet the girls in the park for a picnic which is even nicer!

Need some more tips? Check out these tips to help trim your grocery bill even more!

No Beans about It
Sure, canned beans are pretty cheap but if you look at the price of dried beans, you'll see that it's even cheaper. Even the little things count when it comes to cutting your grocery bills in half. Did you know that you can even cook small beans like lentils in your rice cooker for less than a half an hour?

Cookies! No, Wait... Junk Food!

Cookie recipes are pretty forgiving so you don't have to be a great chef to be able to make a decent/edible batch of cookies. I take it an extra step and make all of our junk food at the house. It cuts on expenses, makes us work for our junk food, is healthier, and is preservative free. Sundays are usually my prep days. I will make and prepackage food for the rest of the week.

If you do decide to buy junk food, portioning it out in reusable bags can help extend the life of that bag of chips and will help with your waist line. If I decide to buy a box of wheat crackers, I read the label and portion out the crackers into serving size baggies. Then I put the baggies back in the box.

So when I am craving something to eat or if I need to pack a quick lunch, I can just grab a baggie and I don't have to worry about how much I am eating. I suggest doing this as soon as you bring your groceries off so you can save time, effort, and to make sure that it really does get done.

Applesauce

If your little kiddo or your pup loves applesauce (let's admit it, even we sneak in a spoon every now and then), you can make homemade applesauce in a crockpot for pennies compared to buying it prepackaged. Not to mention, it is healthier this way as well. No preservatives and no extra sugar!

Just put ten apples (cored, peeled, and diced) and about three fourths of a cup of water in your crockpot. Cook it on high for three to four hours depending on what type of consistency you like. Just make sure to check on it and make sure that it doesn't dry out too much. Add some extra water if it is starting to look a little dry.

If you have some of those baby food jars lying around (I save glass jars to reuse them for crafts or for cooking projects like this. Just make sure that the applesauce has cooled before you spoon it into the jar.

Ricotta Cheese

Yep. Did you know that you can make ricotta cheese at home using a microwave, a glass container, milk, and an acid (I suggest distilled vinegar because it gives you a nice clean flavor with the most tender curds). Just microwave it on high for a couple of minutes, then drain the excess liquid.

Coffee

You can cut your expenses down by hundreds of dollars a year by brewing your own coffee at home instead of going out for a cup of coffee every morning. If you just brew a pot of coffee, you can save money and help the environment by cutting down on your trash output.

Calculate how much you spend on coffee each week. If you are a regular coffee drinker, you probably have one or two cups a day for about five days a week. At five bucks a pop, that's already between $25 and $50 dollars a week! You can spend that money on something else like dinner on the table for your family or perhaps

French Fries

What's cheaper than buying French fries at a fast food place? Buying them in the frozen aisle. What's cheaper than buying them frozen? Making them on your own! Believe it or not, making fries isn't that hard and you can make them out of sweet potatoes for a healthier twist! Just preheat your oven to 375 degrees and cut some potatoes into sticks that are about a fourth of an inch thick. Drizzle some olive oil on them and then bake them for a half an hour. Depending on your oven, they may need to go in for an extra fifteen minutes or so.

Salsa! Ole!

Salsa is pretty easy to make and it is also pretty cheap if you make it from scratch. Since it is so easy, you can play with different recipes and change up the ingredients. Make it as spicy or as thick as you want.

Breakfast is the Best Meal of the Day

Going out for breakfast may be convenient but it is also spendy. It is cheaper to stay at home and make your own English muffin sandwiches, than to buy them at your favorite fast food places. Just buying a carton of eggs, a block of cheese, some ham, and a bag of English muffins (or better yet, make your own batch!); you can make around ten sandwiches for less than having to buy them at three to four dollars a sandwich.

But it's not just breakfast sandwiches. Think granola bars. They are much cheaper and healthier to make from scratch. You can have them for breakfast, grab them for an on-the-go snack, or pack them in your children's lunch boxes. You can make them in different flavors and with different sugar contents. The prepackaged granola bars that you buy in stores are packed full of sugar and preservatives. They can even be upwards of one to two dollars a bar depending on what type of ingredients they come with. Energy bars are more expensive than regular granola bars. You can make energy bars at home too! Check out some easy recipes online.

Conclusion

I hope that you have found this book useful and learnt a few things that will help you cut your outgoings down by a substantial amount.

My goal for you is for you to be able to take that saved money, and use it for good. Whether that is to pay off debt or your mortgage and become financially free, or to pay into a pension scheme to ensure your future, or just to take the kids on holiday. Whatever your goal is, remember pennies add up to pounds and in no time you could have saved a big chunk of cash towards any one of these   things.

Lastly, I want to finish with the penny challenge.

Over the course of one year if you put 1c into a jar on day one, 2c on day two, 3c on day three, a dollar (100c) on day 100 etc etc over the course of the year you will amass $667.95 without barely noticing it. The most you will put into your jar on any one day is $3.65. Probably less than your morning coffee!

Give it a go!

Thank you and good luck!